A

## Marlene Christian

Young Lady mere words
can not express my appreciation
of your interest in my work.
I have enjoyed each conversation
we have shared - May God's
grace continue to rule over
your life. Check out page 30,
I dedicate the Poem, "I Know You"
in your honor. Stay strong, positive,
and focused.
Peace my Sister !! Vincent Espann
August 11, 2000

# A Journey of Transformation

Library of Congress Cataloging-in-Publication Data:

Spann, Vincent E.
A Journey of Transformation – Poems/Vincent E. Spann
p.  cm.
ISBN 0–9678967-0-3
LCCN 00-190122


Published by


## Spider Web Publishing
### Fort Monroe, Virginia

Printed in the United States of America

# A Journey of Transformation

## Poems

# Vincent E. Spann

## Spider Web Publishing
### Fort Monroe, Virginia

# *Dedication*

This book is dedicated to everyone who has impacted my life.  May you stay a flight and soar until your wings grow stronger! Because of you, I shall never be alone.


In loving memory of:
Gussie, Harold, Melain and Anthony Jones
Margaret, Vernon, and Floyd Spann
James and Juanita Taylor
Reverend Floyd R. Gilbert and Thelma "TC" Montgomery

# *Contents*

# *Prelude*

In the winter of 1995, while on a military assignment in South Korea, at Camp Humphreys, I had the divine pleasure of meeting Abigail West, a soldier and aspiring poet. Ms. West displayed a writing style that spoke to my heart as well as my soul. Instantly, I became intrigued and amazed with Ms. West's poetry and writing style. Her writing style inspired my creativity.

Over the years, I have allowed writing poetry to become a gateway. Writing poetry taps into my creative imagination - an imagination driven by a passion to explore and express my thoughts.

This book includes poems that portray those ideas, persons, or places I have encountered while on this pilgrimage. Writing about these encounters has allowed me to show my acknowledgment and appreciation of simple yet inspiring things. I chose these poems because they endorse the joys and pains of love, people, experiences, hope, doubt, gains and losses in life, and spirituality. Furthermore, I am compelled to share with you my idealism, optimism, and the necessity of Christ Jesus. It is my way of sharing a journey of expressions.

My most challenging obstacle was to procure the book's cover. I wanted the cover to show and capture the beauty and spirit of a soul searching for the ultimate transforming experience. An experience that places the soul alongside sand and water, which, for me, is synonymous to the poem "Foot Prints" which is a testament that Christ is always in our midst. The soul in the photograph is without a doubt a soul searching for that ultimate transforming experience.

My next stint was to find such a place, so while on this perennial search I drove upon Fort Monroe. Due to its breathtaking view, I immediately knew this was the place to further share this journey.

I hope this book will enable you to experience this journey with equal depth, height and width as I have. From this point, may the Spirit of God be with you.

*-Vincent E. Spann*

# *Special Acknowledgments*

I thank God for blessing me with this work. Father, I continuously pray that you will forever plant a seed of faith within me. It is because of you that I live. For unto my mother was I conceived, now flesh dwelling.

My mother, Patricia A. Jones-Chambliss; my brother, Olain L. Jones; my sisters, Gussie D. Spann-Jarrett, and Vanessa M. Spann. From the depths of my heart I love and cherish each one of you. Thanks for sharing in this undisturbed family bond.

Gustin Cornelius Smith, a true supporter. Thanks for long hours of listening, spiritual sharing, brotherhood and true, committed friendship. Always remember... Destiny has spoken!

The phoenix, my mentor, M. Rose "Cheley" Barkley; you undoubtedly possess beauty and excellence. You know of no boundaries or limits. May you forever live within me even when your presence is no more. For when that day is come, I shall return to this earth and sprinkle your ashes, so that you rise unto God.

The cameraman, my photographer, Michael T. Tatum; you are truly a man with precision. Your ability to capture beauty and transform it to still photography is a gift that mere words cannot express. I thank you for sharing your gifts. Mr. Tatum's work appears courtesy of Lasting Memories, Hampton, Virginia.

My editors, M. Rose Barkley and Diana McFarland, I sincerely appreciate your contributions. Without your loyal dedication, this book would not have been complete and for this I am deeply grateful.
Ms. Barkley's contributions appear courtesy of Sound Publishing Company.

My best friend, Rodney L. Adams, I am truly your keeper.

My printing team at CSS Publishing, Lima, OH, Mark McCullough, Jeannette Ashby, and Christopher Patton. It was indeed a pleasure working with each of you. I look forward to working with you in the future.

# *Acknowledgments*

Clyde Webster-what manner of man is this that even I answer to?  Please keep believing in me and pushing me to succeed.

Leida Heurtas-Anderson, Linda D. Anderson, Rochelle McCann, David C. Hairston, Terry Witherspoon-Hairston, Robert Johnson, Brenda Shields, Danny Thomas, and Patricia Vaughan, we share an awesome kindred spirit.  Thanks for all your support over the years.  Abide with me!

Reverend John O. Peterson, Male Chorus, Membership Group Twenty and the Alfred Street Baptist Church Family, Alexandria, VA.

The New Mount Olive Baptist Church Family, Hampton, VA

Sally Swan, a skillful librarian and supporter.

Doug Greene of Crippen & Landru, Publishers, a great help in time of need.

Lydia Bailey Brown, a convincing Marketing Professor, thanks for inspiring me to pursue a marketing career.

Yolanda P. Meekie and Tonya Heyward-Reese, thanks for all your assistance.

I also thank my family and friends, especially the McClure, Dozier, Eady, Jones, Lykes, and Taylor Families, Xavier Anderson, Ashara Barner, Joanne Barrett, Robyn Brunicardi, Jimmy Buggs, Jerome Cannon, Robert Carmack, Gary Carpenter, Karmaria Carr, Cedric Carroll, Viola Cash, Ian Chin, Melvina Coakley, Debra Laster-Cousin, LaDonna Davis, Kelleye Mahone-Elmore, Reverend Willie Fleming, John Freeman, Robin Thomas-Freeman, Anthony Grace, Andrea Griffin, Raymond and Debra Hawkins, Michele Hudson, Marcus Hollien, Vincent Hale, Ralph, Sykena, and Jennifer Jarrett, Darlene Jackson, Walter Jenkins, Brenda Jones, Ashley Jones, Olain Jones Jr., Tiara Jones, Thomas Joseph, Jason Lenhardt, Carlton Lee, Leonard Lockett, W. Ray McCollum, Nedrick McDade, Lynda Mills-Tyson, Donald Minus, Chauncey Morris, Celia Morrison, Cathy House-Myers, Orlando Murrell, Teddy Nixon, Elizabeth Palmore, Mary Quick, Sharon Ramsey, James Richard, Robert Riddick, Gregory Shropshire, Josephine Sibley, Donna Simpson, Patricia Smith, Connie Stinson, Kevin Taylor, Boris Terry, Albert F. Thompson, Cecile Torres, Annette and Kiyah Tyler, Dameon Vaughan, Michell Venters, Thomas Walker, Cylethia Pace-Williams, O.J. Williams, Pamela Williams, Dr. Peter Zawadsky, Prince Nelson, Steven Spielberg, Lauryn Hill, Maurice Greene, Jon Drummond, Jack Nicholson, Michael Jordan, Bette Midler, Oprah Winfrey, Vanessa L. Williams, Bebe and Cece Winans, Oleta Adams, Alonzo Mourning, Yolanda Adams, Samuel L. Jackson, Janet Jackson, Jimmy "Jam" Harris III, Terry Lewis, Dr. Martin L. King Jr., Malcolm X, President Abraham Lincoln, President John F. Kennedy, Bessie Smith, and Florence Griffith-Joyner.

P.S. If there is anyone I left out, charge it to my head and not my heart.

# *Inspiring Authors*

Phillis Wheatley (On Being Brought from Africa to America)
Patti LaBelle (Don't Block Your Blessings)
Mark Goulston and Phillip Goldberg (Get Out of Your Own Way)
M. Rose Barkley (Wayfaring Stranger)
Larry Lea (The Hearing Ear)
Lewis B. Smedes (Forgive and Forget)
Dr. Maya Angelou (Wouldn't take Nothing for my Journey)
Susan L. Taylor (In the Spirit)
Iyanla Vanzant (Acts of Faith)
Robert Fulghum
(All I Really Need to Know I Learned in Kindergarten)
E. Lynn Harris (Just as I am)
Lynda LaPlante (Cold Shoulder and Cold Blood)
Barbara Johnson (Splashes of Joy in the Cesspools of Life)
Thich Nhat Hanh (Peace is Every Step)
Melba P. Beals (Warriors Don't Cry)
Connie B. Hooks (Big Girls Don't Cry)
Terry McMillan (Disappearing Act)
Virginia Deberry and Donna Grant
(Tryin' to Sleep in the Bed You Made)
Betty J. Eadie (Embraced by the Light)
Edger Allen Poe (The Tell-Tale Heart)

# A Journey of Transformation

## Poems

# Chapter I
## *Reminiscing*
### *Yesterday's Memories*

# The Poem

A poet
Composer of poetry
Dabbler of simplistic phraseology
Presents me in understandable fashion

I am a verse of great composition
Developed in the mind
Composed in wonderful imagination
The finished product of thought

My beauty of language
My magic of expression
Can be found written in a poem

Prolific writers
Rita Dove
Sandra Gilbert
William Shakespeare
Nikki Giovanni
Robert Graves
Langston Hughes
Drive me to sing unto your soul
Through eloquence and inventive style

I am the island of your most treasured thoughts
I am the unplowed field of your anxieties
I am the recollection of your secret dreams
I am the language you desire to speak

Exhilarate yourself
I am
The poem

# *Yesterday, Today, and Tomorrow*

Yesterday, we cried out with hope that time would pause on our behalf

Still we were ignored

Oftentimes we conferred with God

Asking Him to mend our wounded spirits and ease our pain

To succor us in being victorious in long suffering

By way of love, He heard our cries

Elate yourselves, read of our struggles and achievements

Take heed to our passion for equality, recognition, and prosperity

Go now forth and establish our future

Today, we pause to sound the trumpets, paying tribute to you and your success

We are extremely honored to be your descendants

We are the hope for which you struggled

In unity, we journey on the paths of your accomplishments

We stand firm in our quest for fairness, acceptance, and peace

In brotherhood, we bind our minds never to abdicate our responsibility

To ready our children, our tomorrow

Tomorrow will come, therefore, today I shape my tomorrow

I am a revolution

I vow to carry on the legacy, to always strive to do my best in all my efforts

I will continue to represent my people the best way imaginable

I will accept my trials and tribulations as building blocks to conquer adversity

Serene, I fold my hands and wait, for I too will succeed

For me to know my direction, I must understand my past

In viewing my vast wealth of ancestry, I have only to endeavor

To stop, look, and listen

Clearly, from this point, I stand in full view of my potential

Not lost

Yesterday

Because I see, today

Choices for tomorrow's path

# *Your Blind Faith*

I am

Your offspring

I am

Your child

Don't hide me

In your weakness

Your self-pride

Your self-imposed shackles

Your blind faith

Free your mind

Beyond shallow expectations

Except truth

In order to move forward

Deny me

And I vanish

Uniquely

Incomplete

With celebrated pride

As I

Quietly

Hang

In your blind faith

# They Emerged

Long ago
They emerged
Centered in the crowning glory of liberation
Until riot shook their souls cruel-heartedly

Children seeking knowledge

Around about them
Lingered hatred and cruelty
Yet still
They marched forward
With pride, strength and determination
Conquering
Disorder

Children seeking knowledge

Today
They assemble to celebrate their victory
By and by
They gather in harmony
Unceasingly unified

Celebrating knowledge

History honors them
As an educated combined force
They emerged
All nine
They emerged
with courage, intelligence, and self-respect

Sharing knowledge

# *Pride*

Beat it down
I say
Beat it down

Pride

Beat it down

Let it not
Slowly
Smoothly
Waltz upon
Your happiness
Rob you
Of your journey
Your destiny
           Be thou modest

Beat it down
I say
Beat it down

Pride

Beat it down

Let it not
Hinder the process
By which
You manifest
Your happiness

Your joy
Your evolution

        Be thou modest
Beat it down
I say
Beat it down

Pride

Beat it down

Force it
From the pit of your belly
Let it not
Suck away
Your peace of mind
Your ability to forgive
Your need to forget
        Be thou modest
        Modest
        Thou must be
        To
Beat it down
Pride
Beat it down
And move on

# *Missed Opportunity*

If the sun hadn't been shining in your eyes
I would have ignored
Your endless kindness
Your timeless patience
Your inviting spirit

It's been awhile since the sun has given a twinkle
to mine eyes

And to imagine…

If the sun hadn't been shining in your eyes
I would have ignored
Your wholesome sincerity
Your wise courage
Your genuine purpose

I tell you the truth

This is the simple truth

It's been awhile since the sun has given a twinkle
to mine eyes

Just think…

What would have happened

If the sun hadn't been shining in your eyes

# Chapter II
*Icons*
*Validation!*

# *My Brother's Keeper*

I am his Keeper

> I keep him
> Strong
> Growing
> Spiritual
> Supported

My brother; he is kept

I am his Keeper

> I keep him
> Loyal
> Sincere
> Valued
> Faultless

My brother; he is kept

I am his Keeper

> I keep him
> Shielded
> Protected
> Preserved
> Guarded

My brother; he is kept

I am his Keeper

I keep him
Remarkable
Regal
Unafraid
Guided

My brother; he is kept

I am his Keeper

I keep him
Immovable
Steadfast
Abounding
Dwelling
Godly

He is kept

I am the keeper
Of my brother
I keep him

My brother; he is kept

# I Know U

I know U

The essence of being
Portraying Ebony on the rise
Turning heads with your grace and style
Standing firm in your haughty ways
A memorizing blessing

I know U

Ms. Mocha
Ms. Sable
Ms. Raven
Ms. Bronze
Spanning the Shades
Sultry earth tones

I know U

Exciting in all you do
Teasing me with your intellect, wisdom, faith and charm
I honor you
Intrigued and enraptured with what I see
Perfection at work
Charismatic in your talk
Strengthen your stride
Strut Sheba
Stroll as you please
I pay tribute to you in varying degrees

I know U

My sister
My friend
Be true to yourself
Most importantly be proud of who you are
An African-American Queen
Bone of my brothers
Flesh of my brothers
Strength of my brothers
Pride of my brothers

I Know U

# *Thyself*

Go my child

Yonder

Search the world over

Rid Thyself

Find Thyself

Teach Thyself

Study Thyself

Transmute Thyself

Perfect Thyself

Know Thyself

Believe Thyself

Love Thyself

Limit Not Thyself

Market Thyself

Never stop

Transcending

My child

# My Mother's Womb

Womb
My Mother's
My siblings lived
Protected
No fears
No thank you
No please
They complained
Complained
Complained

My mother, Pat, a gentle woman
Would lose her cool
"Stop moving," she would yell
My siblings, ignored her
They kicked, moved, rebelled
Unrestrained kids
Made her pregnancy a living pit

My older brother, Nut
Too demanding
"Feed me," he would shout
I'm hungry
I'm want my bottle
I'm undernourished

My eldest sister, Gussie
Too whiny
"Turn on the lights," she would cry
Turn down the heat
I need some air
I can't sleep

My youngest sister, Pig
A Stellar
"Where is the sun," she would grumble
Where are the birds
Where are the flowers
Where are the trees

Then there's me, Whistle
Extremely caring
"Mother," I would whisper
Rest
Exercise
Sleep

Womb
My Mother's
A place where memories reside
A place of solace
A place of joy
A house of style

# *He Returned*

Profusely sweating yet controlled
He came forth panting
Taken back from death
Many years succeeding his untimely demise

He returned

He appeared different in unrecognizable beauty
He wore a trite overcoat
His graying wool hair neatly dreaded
His feet shining like bronze
His spirit refreshed, transformed and emancipated

He returned

While reaching for me
He frightened me
When I could bare no more
I turned away
I controlled myself
Reflected on him
I remembered him

He returned

I turned slowly to face him
I reached for him
He disappeared
Then I awakened
To find him
Dead
My drug-addicted neighbor

He returned
In the mind of a poet
He returned

# *Trigger*

Life-threatening
Silver
Steel
Unsteady
Explosive
Discharging
Powerful
Trigger

Abandoned
On my own
Drifting
Daily
Hunting
Victims
Reckless
Trigger

Shot his brother
Shot your sister
In cold blood
Headlines
Trigger
Fired
Two shots
Killing him
Killing her

Trigger
Out of control
Misused
Shot a child
Impairing
Yours
Brady Bill

Trigger
Arrested
Booked
Tried
Guilty
Sentenced
Locked away
In safekeeping

# *That Dog*

Get that dog out of this house

He belongs
Outside
So that he may rove
In his natural
Habitat
Instead
He's in here
Jumping on the bed
Messing up the sheets

Get that dog out of this house

Barking
All times of the night
Running
Up and down the stairs
Drinking
Water from the toilet
Thirsty
For attention

Get that dog out of this house

Forever lurking around
Sniffing
Stealing
My favorite toys

**A Journey of Transformation**

Gnawing
On my favorite slippers
Infinitely
Leaving the fibers
Laying about

Get that dog out of this house

Leaving
His load of rubbish
All over the place
Smelling like he wants to be alone
Playing in my litter box
Oftentimes
Intimidating me

Get that dog out of this house

You
Claim
He's your best friend
Who am I
Either
He goes or I go
I am the coolest Cat alive
And I get no respect
All because of
That Dog

This is your last warning

Get that dog out of this house

# Optimistic Tears

Morning

Outside

Sitting

Dreading the heat

Sun

Scorching

Sweaty

Heat rays

Dancing

Afternoon

Premonition

Forecast

Slight chance of showers

Sitting

Now still

Feeling

Optimistic

Evening

Blinking

Eyes

Composure lost

Sun

Fading

Tears

Falling

Rain

Dripping

Wet

Sky

Determined

Cloud

Shaded

Sun

Optimistic

Reality

Your

Defeat

Refreshing

# Chapter III
## *Joys and Pains*
### *Coming soon*

# In Each Other's Heart

Frustrated
At odds
Yet searching for tolerance

We traveled by train
In dark hours
Hoping to see our way

       Our hearts pounding
       Boom
       Boom

Two souls traveling
Aggressively seeking love's contractual agreement
A form of connection

Last stop
The peaceful village
Heartsville

A city of hope
A city of understanding
Where love endlessly flows and tolerance reigns

       Our hearts pounding
       Boom
       Boom

As the train skids to the last stop
I shout, "Hold Me"
My lover, companion, friend
Gird your fears
Detrain with me

Head that way
Quickly
So that we reach our destination
The place we belong
In each other's

Heart

Pounding

Boom

Boom

# Stand With Me

Come stand with me beneath the drenched willow tree
near the Bayou.

And while the tree's shadow protects us from the liquid
sunshine, which drips endlessly, I'll provide you cover while my
love shields you from the rain.

And while standing with me, listen softly as the raindrops play a
sweet, sweet melody.

For at this precise moment, you shall come to know that our
togetherness is concealed by the innermost part of our
commitment, when it's stormy outside.

Matters not the weather
Come stand with me always.

# The Act Played Out

Eyes
Met
Collaboration
Shared
Successfully

Act played out

Analysis
Secret
Exposed
Appetite
Fulfilled

Act played out

Temples
Sweaty
Turning point
Uncovered
Lacking dryness

Act played out

Shaking
Uncontrollably
Helplessly
Embarrassed
Bodies
Stimulated

Act played out

Performance
Riveting
Thrilling
Fulfilling
Completely
Satisfied

Act played out

# Call Me, I Will Listen

Where are you
I'm thinking of you
I'm dreaming of you
Awakening to discover you missing
Craving to be where you are
What are your thoughts
Call me
I will listen


Lend me an ear
I need you to hear me
My life revolves around you
During the times I shared with you, you became everything
Through our giving we cared for each other
When desire came upon us we touched, kissed, embraced
You said you would always care for me
You said you would always be near
But you've gone astray
I long to hear your explanation
Call me
I will listen


It was you who said we had a unique love
What happened
Why did you change
Why did you leave me in the dark
What a strange way to show your commitment
Tell me, how did I lose you
I'm entitled to an explanation
What wrong did I do
Call me
I will listen

When you changed, I didn't know
if I would live another second
Can you imagine a man not knowing if he will live
It is devastating
The day you changed, I returned my broken heart
Which till this day silently pumps my love for you
I am suffering
But what do you care
You're not here
What wisdom can you offer
Call me
I will listen
Call me
I will listen
Listen
Listen
Do you not hear me calling

# *Oh Wretched Love*

Oh Wretched Love, my heart did thou stealeth,
I slumber in emptiness

Behold, sun of my soul, thou art unfair,
I gleam no more for thou hast faded away

And hath taken away thy presence,
Where might I find thee

Oh Wretched Love, thou hast seized my loving kindness,
I trusted thee like a thief in the night

Thou hast crushed my heart under thy feet,
I count the scattered pieces

Thou hast crumbled my love,
I shall gather the fragments that remain

Oh Wretched Love, acknowledge my plea,
come not near unto me.
Verily I say unto thee, I've forgiven thee and thy ways

Therefore, stand still, and keep watch
For when the time cometh

I shall inherit my dignity-how glorious

I shall delight myself in the abundance of
serenity-how miraculous

I shall soon bear this hurt no more-how victorious

Oh Wretched Love
Wretched Love
Arise! See the wondrous change in me

# What Happened to You Loving Me

Like a beating heart
Rapidly you returned to me
Only this time smitten with my life
Kindly you offered comfort, understanding, and compassion
Behind the scenes you brewed another clever and cruel scheme

Silly
Troubled me
An unconscious being
Continuously, I exhausted my time and energy pleasing you
Gave you free will to entertain me as you pleased
Never once did I questioned your actions

What happened to you loving me

I rearranged my style to satisfy your expectations
I wanted you to take notice-be proud of me
So I spent every Tuesday through Saturday reinventing myself
Only for you to show your disapproval on Sundays

Silly
Troubled me
My friends struggled to warn me
But nothing would prepare me for the shock
You delivered on Monday
With your vicious never-ending blows and ridicule
You caught me off guard with your physical and emotional abuse
Your inability to appreciate my self-worth and me

What happened to you loving me

I thought I was needed
I thought I was cherished
I thought I was loved
My, my, my
Was I unwise and blind

Silly
Troubled me
Had the audacity to put off unleashing my soul
From your hostile and sadistic behavior
Thought I could change you
Believed your violence would subside
I wanted you to adore me

What happened to you loving me

But you've destroyed this passion
And it's high time I free this ridiculous notion I have of
Love
Value and Unity

My greatest joy is to forget everything encompassed
In your hostile mistreatment
A behavior inundated with
Pain
Cruelty and embarrassment

But this day, I beseech you, my fallen angel
Nothing you utter can keep me from my freedom
I will recover my dignity and self-esteem
But before I go I must reveal...

I know what happened to you loving me
You never loved yourself

A Journey of Transformation          57

# *Chapter IV*
## *P-Mail*
### *(Poetic Mail)*

# ANGRILY DEVASTATED
120 South Two-Mile Shore
River City, Virginia  12096

January 20, 1996

SUBJECT:  Remembering

Helpless Fate
120 Golden Street View
Golden City, Heaven  12086

Dear Fate,

For years I have been missing you!  And I must know to what extent do you think of me.  Furthermore, I want to ask you a few questions.

Do you remember when we sat alone in my yacht at sea, talking, thinking and kissing?  And that we would soon set sail to our final destination, the end of the shore?  Do you remember approaching the seashore and a great wave appeared causing us to face danger?  Do you remember?

Fate, I remember!  I remember my yacht capsizing.  I remember the waters whisking you away, seeing your lips move but to no avail.  I remember seeing you overtaken by the evil wave breaking on the shore.  Can you ever forgive me for being so helpless in your defeat?

Fate, ten years later, time slowly passes and I still visit the seashore. These days I sit alone, lost and confused. While sitting there, I recall your last spoken phrase, "This passion is awful and what happened to the kiss?" At this moment, I'm still mending my broken spirit. Truth be told, my heart often agonizes over the pain I must live with. Considering all, I still find time to smile and relive the way we were. I routinely reminisce with memories of your spirit.

My dearest Fate, if for any reason, you decide to return to the seashore, remember I'll be there waiting, thinking, alone. I miss you terribly!

Sincerely,


**Angrily Devastated**

# OLD MAN MARTIN
1947 Unity Street
Golden City, Heaven  22797

---

February 27, 1997


REMINDER FOR ALL


SUBJECT:  Unity

Dear Citizens,

For the past fifty years, I have observed you in your quest to attain unity.  During last year's Black History Month observance you promised to rise above the obstacles that cause separation.  On one accord, you agreed on making the bonding process more practical.  Remember the individual standing amongst you shouting, "The time for change was yesterday and the time to unite is now?"  You have to admit; the individual's outcry was a wake-up call of Oneness for All.

It is imperative that you continue to strengthen your unification and improve the process, in which you endeavor to accomplish this goal.  Without this, unity cannot be achieved.  In the long run, you have to ask yourselves, "When it comes to unity, are you better off today than you were fifty years ago?"  There are certain individuals who will disagree with you when you say, "Yes". Therefore, it is up to them to sit down and listen to your reasons, explaining why you feel you are better off today.

Remember that Unity begins with self; therefore, act responsibly so that you may successfully seek oneness with others.

Sincerely,

*Old Man Martin*

**DROWNING SOUL**
8299 Water Shore Avenue
Seaside, Galilee 80299

August 2, 1999

LETTER FOR MY SAVIOR

SUBJECT:  Drowning

Dear Lord,

  I have visited this seashore many times, praying that you
would soon bless me.  I believed that no matter how much I
doubted you, you would still come forth and pour out a blessing.
But when mid-day fell, I didn't sense your presence.  You
seemed so far away.

  My fears overcame me.  I felt betrayed and vexed.  I felt
defeated.  I had nowhere to run.  I had no one to talk to.  I had
weak faith and strength; therefore, I could not lift up mine eyes
and seek thee.

  I went astray.  I walked alone by the waters.  I walked with my
fears.  Moreover, I was tossed with the wind.   At that moment
the waters began to consume me.  While on a downward spiral,
I felt death's presence.  I spent endless time sinking in my fears,
drowning in a dangerous shifting sea.  I sank deeper and lower
without peace.

Yet, while in my distress, I cried unto thee, "Incline your ear, and come for me. My lungs are full of water, and my life draweth unto the grave. Do not turn away, stretch forth thy hand and rescue me. Hear, O Lord, my plea. Show thy compassion, save me, so that I may glorify thy name daily."

Behold, all praises to you, my Lord, with a strong hand you have recovered me. And from this day forward I shall tell the world of your grace and mercy.

Sincerely,

**Drowning Soul**

# JESUS CHRIST
1999 Knowledge Street
Golden City, Heaven 81199

August 11, 1999

LETTER FOR ALL WHO SEEK ME

SUBJECT: Things you should know

Dear Child,

For years you have been confused and lacking in your understanding. Today, I shall help you unfold the mystery of your confusion. I shall help you to find your way. I will start from A and finish with Z. My word of caution to you is that you come to me with your ears wide open.

On this day, you shall no longer think of bread when I say unto you, "Watch out for the yeast of Satan. But in the fullness thereof, you shall think on agitation, unrest and sin."
When I say unto you, "The individuals you encounter- what are their thoughts concerning me?" You will utter, "Well, he certainly was not John the Baptist, nor was he
a prophet, but in my heart, he is the Son of God. He is my Lord and Savior Jesus Christ. He is the one coming to claim this world and me."

On the second day, when questioned, "Does God hear a sinner when he or she prays?" Shout, "Surely! He heard me! He saved me! And forgave me!"

In addition, you are to love one another just as my Father loves you. You must learn to forgive and forget. Likewise, flee hatred; it hinders your willingness to love.

Furthermore, know this, you are to continue to study to show thyself affirmed by my Father. For your work will surely be examined. Therefore, know what my Father's word says and proposes. You are to teach His word! You are to live by His word! Shortly, heaven and earth will pass, but my Father's word will remain true and unchanged!

Sincerely,


*The Lord Jesus Christ*

# Chapter V
## Going through the change
Fortitude strengthens our mind as we face
adversity with courage

# *For Nothing Matters*

Nothing matters at all

It matters not

Not at all

For nothing matters

No matter what happens

It will not matter

For nothing matters

Not even the things that matter

Or

Does it matter

You must

Decide

# *Peaceful Waters*

Relaxing
Along

Peaceful
Waters

Eyes
Closed

Quietly
Meditating

Thoughts
Centered

On
Christ

Concentration
Interrupted

Familiar
Silhouette

Approaching
Slowly

Walking
Upon

Water
Waves

Hands
Stretched

Beckoning
Come

Walk
Upon

These
Waters

With
Me

Trust
Obey

Faithfully
Believe

Peaceful
Waters

Will
Flow

Till
We

Reach
Zion

The
City

Of
Our

Great
Kings

# *Engaged*

Already night forty
5 point 5 seconds after midnight
I had been in exile with my work
Man, was I hungry

Although I stood alone in my kitchen
I sensed I wasn't on my own
I felt movement
So I turned slowly and found him
Peering in my half shut window

He wore a red P-coat
Black beret and matching scarf
He startled me with his sly grin and chipped teeth
But due to my curiosity and his tempting aura
I felt compelled to entertain him

Within minutes, I found myself engaged
Engaged with a smooth talker
Man, could he talk

We talked at great length of my work
He promised to produce, market and publish my poetry
If I would bow down and worship him
In that moment
I knew he was up to no good

Instantly, I turned to face him
I shouted, "Get from behind me, I serve the Lord God only"
I ordered him to the door
As soon as he moved into position
I kicked him with force I didn't know existed

The impact threw him high
The pavement landing was hard
His face displayed disgust and anger
Seconds passed before his beret came spiraling down from
mid-air
Landing on his ego

The deceiver got up
Dusted himself
Pushed me down
Laughed uncontrollably
Shouted, "I'll be back"
Clapped his hands and vanished

Just as I started to get up
Jesus appeared and ministered to me
He looked upon me
Held me tight
Then whispered, "Great looking armor, you wear it well,
and as I promised, ye shall receive the crown of life!"

# *Wash My Feet*

Savior
Near the stone upon the sand
Plant my wandering feet in the interior walls of the water
Let your angels camp about me keeping watch
Draw nigh Lord
Make thy presence known
Wash my feet
Purify me with hyssop
Give me perfect peace to sojourn

Lord
Keep my feet
Wash my feet
Strengthen my feet
Order my steps
For I seek a holy walk

Savior
Lead me
Down a righteous path
Come evening and dawn and mid-day
My feet will dance unto thee
Giving praise
Upon the sand where you carry me

Lord
Keep my feet
Wash my feet
Strengthen my feet
Order my steps
For I seek a holy walk

Savior
Bless me
Come
Walk with me
While I tarry
Near the stone upon the sand

# High of Low Times

Master
Keep me
Cold winds
Blowing
In thee I put my trust

Father
Keep
Thy promises
In hardship
Poverty
High of low times
When I'm weak
Strengthen me

Master
Free me
Worries
Close at hand
Troubles
Blowing
I'm afraid

Father
Keep
Thy promises
In disbelieving
Fear
High of low times
I'm weak
Strengthen me

Master
Times are hard
All alone
Life's struggles
Facing
Privately
Lord
I need a friend
Where are you
I'm afraid

Father
Keep
Thy promises
In distress
Sadness
Heartbreaks
High of low times
I'm weak
Strengthen me

Master
Be with me
When I awaken
When my head is lifted high
And I'm sobbing
For what reason
Father
For what reason

Father
Comfort me
In the
High of Low times

# *Alone with Thee in Thy Presence*

Holy Spirit
Come nigh unto me
I hunger to be one with thee
Let me taste thy presence

Each time I open the door unto you
I become nobler
Concealed
Undisturbed
With love overflowing

When thy presence is upon me
My heart learns reverence
My soul is unhindered
Salvation flows in my veins

When I receive thy grace
Your peace rules
Your power procures me
Your faithful love mollifies me
I capitalize on your presence

When I'm alone in your presence
My faith waivers not
You grant me serenity
When I become one with thee
Alone with thee in thy presence

# My Good and Faithful Servant

Enter the gate
North side of the Alter
Upon which the blood was sprinkled
Enter therein
Be blessed

On the first day
Possess the Spirit
For it rests on the region, that far South
Go now
Fetching
Stop by the burning bush
Remove thy shoes
Greet Moses - the Guard
Render a salute to Noah - the Captain

On the second day
Greet the beloved of the Middle Passage
Already settled in the East
Fellowship with the queen - Mary mother of Jesus
Pray with Job - undoubtedly a conqueror
Find Isaac - a lamb without blemish
Sing hallelujah with Michael - the archangel

A Journey of Transformation

On the third day
Travel two thousand feet along the coastal region, that far
West
Meet the Shepherd - most treasured Psalms
The only Begotten
Crucified
Resurrected
Savior of the world
Christ Jesus
Lord of Lords
The light of our salvation

On the fourth day
Be not afraid
Judgment cometh
Meet God the Father
A day of Pentecost
Validation of faith
Receive the reward
Well done
My Good and Faithful Servant
Well done

# *Under the Shadows of Your Wings*

Sovereign Lord

Under the shadows of your wings
I take refuge
For I am a veteran of fear

Redeemer

Let thy fragrance pamper my senses
In a compelling way
Intrigue me with thy closeness

Creator

Under the shadows of your wings
Teach me thy way
For I long to study thee

Master

Give ear to my words
Hide not thyself from me
I genuinely seek thee

My King

Under the shadows of your wings
I relinquish all
Take unto thee my inheritance

Counselor

In the midst of troubles
Shield me
Calm the storms

My God

Under the shadows of your wings
I am free
Satan no longer controls me
As long as I abide
Under the shadows of your wings

# The Journey

In the distance lies the unknown
A hazy pilgrimage
One of great trials and tribulations
A journey often traveled
One requiring endurance and strength

To survive
You must overcome
Victoriously
You must conquer

Take on adversity
Dread nothing
Fear nothing
Have faith in God

Manifest your strength
Flaunt your Endurance
Your determination
Your bravery

Remain steadfast
Stand still
Display courage
Meet the challenge

Overtake misfortunes
Successfully
Finish the course
For in the end
Fortitude will bring you through
The Journey

# *Transformation*

A process, which compels you to change
your state of being, environment, or personality;
It's the very act you commit
at that moment you are changed.


## *Vincent E. Spann*

# Interlude

In the Spirit of God
Faith is the inevitable
It is your failure to believe that hinders your growth
Do not go on robbed of your blessings
Have no doubts


## Vincent E. Spann

# *Poetry Log*

"Yesterday, Today, and Tomorrow" written February 28, 1996
"Your Blind Faith" written October 2, 1999
"They Emerge" written September 16, 1999
"The Poem" written October 8, 1999
"Pride" written January 1, 2000
"Missed Opportunity" written December 31, 1999

"My Brother's Keeper" written January 28, 1995
"I Know You" written March 9, 1995
"Thyself" written January 15, 1999
"My Mother's Womb" written March 30, 1995
"He Returned" written August 16, 1999
"Trigger" written October 20, 1997
"That Dog" written August 13, 1999
"Optimistic Tears" written October 8, 1997

"In Each Others Heart" written January 16, 1999
"Stand With Me" written July 27, 1998
"The Act Played Out" written September 1, 1998
"Call me, I Will Listen" written February 13, 1995
"Oh Wretched Love" written June 10, 1998
"What Happened To You Loving Me" written March 4, 2000

"Remembering" written January 20, 1996
"Unity" written February 27, 1997
"Drowning Soul" written August 2, 1999
"Things You Should Know" written August 11, 1999

"Nothing Matters" written January 17, 1999
"Peaceful Waters" written March 6, 2000
"Engaged" written October 9, 1999
"Wash My Feet" written August 1, 1999
"High of Low Times" written August 5, 1999
"Alone In His Presence" written August 3, 1999
"My Good and Faithful Servant" written August 7, 1999
"Under The Shadows Of Your Wing" written August 5, 1999
"The Journey" written January 6, 1995

# E Mail Address

Send Your comments to:

Spiderwebpublishing @ home.com

## OR

Spiderwebpublishing@yahoo.com